Tadpole Books are published by Jump!, 5357 Penn Avenue South, Minneapolis, MN 55419, www.jumplibrary.com

Copyright ©2024 Jump. International copyright reserved in all countries. No part of this book may be reproduced in any form without written permission from the publisher.

**Editor:** Jenna Gleisner  **Designer:** Emma Almgren-Bersie  **Translator:** Annette Granat

**Photo Credits:** Konstantin Novikov/Shutterstock, cover; frantisekhojdysz/Shutterstock, 1; Beto Bormann/iStock, 2tl, 4–5; Hannes Klostermann/Alamy, 2tr, 12–13; Howard Chen/iStock, 2ml, 6–7; Nature Picture Library/Alamy, 2mr, 10–11; Tomas Kotouc/Shutterstock, 2bl, 14–15; EXTREME-PHOTOGRAPHER/iStock, 2br, 8–9; Jsegalexplore/Shutterstock, 3; Oleg Kovtun Hydrobio/Shutterstock, 16tl; SaltedLife/Shutterstock, 16tr; Jesus Cobaleda/Shutterstock, 16bl; Katerina Maksymenko/Shutterstock, 16br.

Library of Congress Cataloging-in-Publication Data is available at www.loc.gov or upon request from the publisher.
ISBN: 979-8-88996-738-5 (hardcover)
ISBN: 979-8-88996-739-2 (paperback)
ISBN: 979-8-88996-740-8 (ebook)

MIS PRIMEROS LIBROS DE ANIMALES

# LOS TIBURONES

por Natalie Deniston

## TABLA DE CONTENIDO

**Palabras a saber**......................2
**Los tiburones**........................3
**¡Repasemos!**........................16
**Índice**...............................16

# PALABRAS A SABER

aletas

branquias

cola

dientes

hocico

ojos

# LOS TIBURONES

Un tiburón nada.

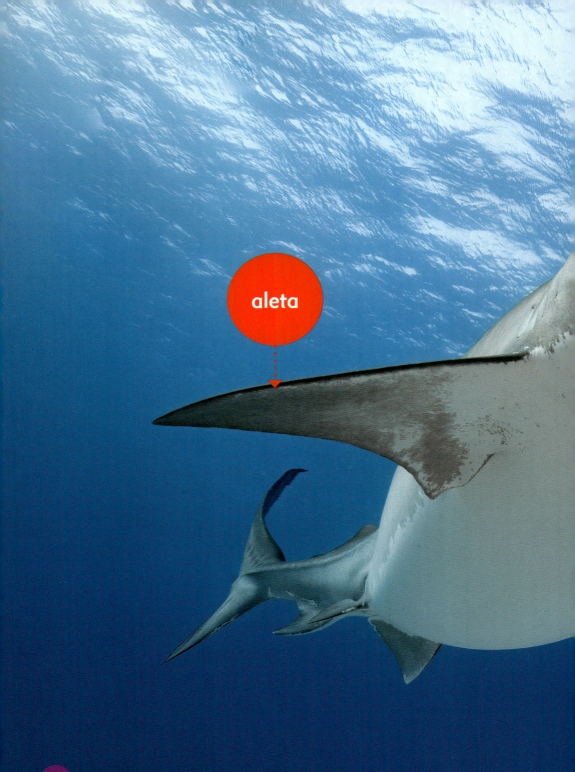

Él tiene aletas.

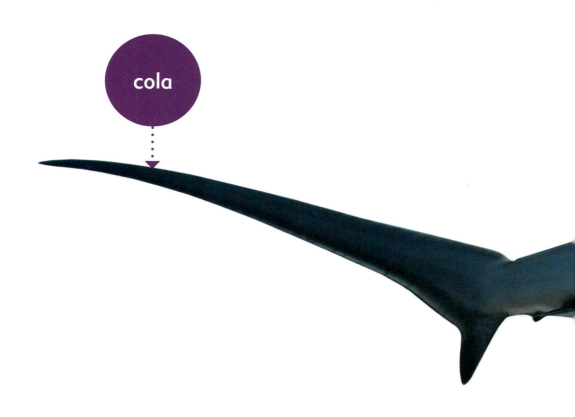

**Tiene una cola.**

ojo

Tiene ojos.

hocico

**Tiene un hocico.**

## ¡REPASEMOS!

Los tiburones son peces. Ellos nadan en el océano. Respiran por sus branquias. Apunta hacia otros tipos de peces que ves abajo.

## ÍNDICE

aletas 5            hocico 15
branquias 13        nada 3
cola 7              ojos 9
dientes 11